MOM'S GREAT ADVICE FOR TEENS

Advice Every Teen Needs For Rewarding Adolescence

By

Nancy Hector

Copyright

DEDICATION

This book is dedicated to everyone who has ever made a good difference in my life throughout my adolescence, especially my father and mother, Mr. and Mrs. Walter Hawkins. Also, a special thanks to my husband Smith.

Table of contents

Chapter 13: Accessing accurate information about others:

Conclusion

Introduction

When children first become teens, they are eager to explore life and make the most of it. Unfortunately, the childhood defined by so many fantasies differs greatly from this new stage. Peer pressure, challenges in selecting friends, coping with self-esteem, self-care, dealing with self-images imposed by teen physical changes, and so on begin. Being an adolescent is a period of immense transition. Teenage years are among the scariest, horrifying, exhilarating, and optimistic of our life. It's a period of blunders, embarrassing situations, having no idea but believing we're omniscient, and having more fun and drama in a few short years than we would have in any other decade of our life.

Summer is something we speak about all year as adolescents! We eagerly await the conclusion of it and diligently count down the days. However, there will come a time when summer will not be distinguished from the other seasons, which is one of the nicest aspects of being a teenager. Finding a sense of meaning in life is a journey for teenagers. Teens are advised to take their time. Be patient if they seem stuck, and realize that life is an ever-changing process. Teens should take their time in determining their life purpose; it is acceptable to not have all of the answers right immediately.

Being a teenager allows you to discover who you are. Being a teenager is wonderful because it is the one moment in our lives when we may discover a happy medium between childhood and maturity. We can blame our immaturity for our infantile behavior, yet we still play the 'I am almost an adult' card when it is convenient. Sometimes we may approach adulthood without taking on all of the obligations that come with it. The benefit of being a teenager is that you have greater leeway to make errors. Because you haven't fully developed common sense, you're unlikely to be penalized for not knowing better. As a result, adolescence is a learning process that may be considered practice before you enter the actual world on your own. Mistakes are okay, but what if these errors have resulted in irreversible damages?

Nancy Hector, the author, is a mother of three children, two of whom are adolescents. She has learned a lot about teens over the years, having worked in many venues that allowed her to interact with them directly. She grew up in an environment in which we as parents influence children's everyday life. She is fortunate to have lived with a mother and father, as well as other relatives who are also parents in a large family. Her birth parents were never solely responsible for her upbringing; rather, it was a collaborative effort of my parents throughout life. Though it was challenging to have so many people telling you what to do, it was worthwhile because parents perceive things in ways that kids do not.

When I was a teenager, having a parent or any of the grown-ups continually telling me what to do was difficult, but I still thought that the pieces of wisdom they offer children, particularly adolescents, come straight from what life has taught them as adults when they were teens. As an adult, I realize what my parents were attempting to teach me. Then I can firmly tell the present generation that there is a lot more life beyond adolescence and that greater preparation for a better life is unavoidable. The majority of the teachings we require to prepare us for the difficult life out there are geared toward us while we are teenagers.

This book provides advice that every great mother should give to their adolescent children to prepare them for the life that awaits them. So, are you a teen seeking advice from experienced parents, or are you a teen struggling to adjust to the new life that awaits you after childhood? This is the book for you. This book will provide you with motherly guidance and show you how to overcome the bulk of the issues that today's youngsters are confronted with. Are you a mother looking to improve your parenting skills by understanding your teen's behavior and directing them correctly without conflict? Then this book is for you as well. This book provides parenting ideas that a mother may offer to acquire images and help them get the best out of the adolescent, who will eventually grow into a better young adult. So, what are you holding out for? Get this book right away and start living up to your full potential. If you're a mother, grab this book and be the greatest parent you can be for your child.

Chapter 1: Never Compare Yourself to others

If you continuously compare yourself to others, you will never find out who you are. When you look to others to assess your value, you are disregarding your abilities, physical traits, and voice. Instead, focus your efforts on learning all your abilities, expanding on your strengths, and fine refining those deficiencies. Honor who you were intended to be, and spend your life appreciating your particular features and unique sense of purpose. Be the best you, as that's enough. Realize why you are locked in the game of comparison. You need to consider why you feel the need to compare yourself to other people and how it could be affecting you. By acknowledging these facts, you'll be able to move ahead and stop wasting your time with comparisons. Rather than getting trapped worrying about how you measure up, embrace who you are. Think about what you can do for other people and what type of person you want to be. Focus on it instead of what everyone else is doing. If we all think about how we can assist others and be our best selves, the world can become a lot better fairly rapidly. Realize that idealizing someone is unreasonable. We just concentrate on particular features of the person we idealize, and they become a grandiose illusion that we construct. We select simply to look at those aspects we idealize while we reject other characteristics that were not attractive to us.

You should evaluate what you are role modeling as an adolescent. Are you comparing yourself to others, making remarks about how you wish you were someone different than you are? The greatest path to a full existence is to appreciate what you have rather than concentrate on what you're missing. Model this mindset to make you feel the same.

Replace negative ideas with good ones. When you compare yourself with others, you may regard yourself poorly. If you have negative ideas about yourself, remind yourself to turn those thoughts into something you are proud of.

Chapter 2: Pick your friends wisely

During the adolescent years, friendships are vital for various reasons. Teenagers often spend more time with their friends than they do with their parents, siblings, or other social acquaintances. Therefore, buddies impact many facets of a teenager's life. Healthy friendships may help youngsters avoid misbehavior, loneliness, and many of the bad qualities that are linked with this phase of life.

Healthy friendships make youngsters feel accepted and confident and may pave the path for the formation of additional beneficial social relationships. Confidence and feeling accepted are key attributes for a teen's social and emotional growth. When a youngster feels as though he is a member of a group, he is less likely to be adversely impacted by bullying and other types of rejection. Teens who feel secure and accepted may also be less inclined to partake in the bullying of others. Friends may have helpful effects on the educational, social, and personal elements of a teenager's life. Because friends generally have the same objectives and/or interests, they may convince a kid to make excellent choices. They may reduce misbehavior and conflict, support achievement in school, and offer the foundation for a bigger network of relationships that will be advantageous later in life. Friendships may also assist a kid get back on track with her goals and/or plans for the future when other, more negative influences are present.

The adolescent years are typically difficult. Having trustworthy, loyal friends is vital to help youngsters cope with the stress and uncertainty that is a typical part of growth. As highlighted by adolescent expert Maria de Guzman, "healthy friendships offer youngsters social support for coping with some of the obstacles of adolescence." Friends may act as a sounding board for concerns such as relationships, school, employment, and conflict with parents. Friends are also sources of pleasure and excitement. Friendships or peer groups help teens discover healthy ways to have fun outside of family, school, and employment. With toxic peer influences, an adolescent may engage in undesirable conduct. Healthy friendships, on the other hand, foster interests that do not include the danger of delinquency or injury. An essay uploaded to the University of Illinois Extension indicates that, via companionship, leisure, and mutual objectives, friendships foster joy and excitement.

Chapter 3: Always make time for self-care

It's so easy to forget that we need to make time for ourselves. Self-care looks different to everyone, so as you learn to know yourself better, tune into what you need to be well, both physically and emotionally. Don’t deny yourself this crucial luxury. If you don’t refresh your mental and physical well-being, the results may be devastating. Find methods to relax and recharge both your body and mind. Then practice them consistently. Find healthy strategies to deal with stress. Stress is a continual issue that we all have to cope with. If we do not discover healthy methods in which to manage our everyday stresses, they may wind up having a toll on our physical and mental health. If you've tried some or all of the strategies above and are still having trouble coping with stress, you may want to speak to an empathetic person, such as a friend, family member, or therapist, to get the support you need to start experiencing a more calm state of mind, even in the middle of an otherwise chaotic existence.

Manage duties. Use a calendar or planning tool to keep track of assignments, chores, practices, and other commitments. Of course, planning is of little use if you don't accomplish what you intend. Managing stress also entails frequent studying, staying on top of work, and fighting procrastination. Take time to ponder a little every day and think about how things are going. What do you need to work on, accomplish, or make time for?

Avoid emotional eating. When we are stressed out, we often have a propensity to attempt to soothe ourselves by eating unhealthy meals, which simply leads to bad sentiments about ourselves later. Become more careful of your eating patterns when you are dealing with pressure, and keep some nutritious snacks on hand to fall back on rather than grabbing for another doughnut or cookie.

Engage in physical exercise several times a week. Going for a jog or working out are fantastic strategies to get rid of excessive tension. If you don't have time to go to the gym, take a stroll around the block during your lunch hour. Moving our bodies may keep us physically fit and healthy, which can help us feel better emotionally as well.

Create a healthy relationship with technology: Understanding how you use technology is the first step to creating a healthy relationship. Gauge how much time you're spending on each application and adapt your approach appropriately. Turn off superfluous alerts, restrict your screen time habits, advocate a no-technology zone while pals are present, mute and ban unfavorable accounts, and ultimately adopt media agreements. If you're monitoring your children's digital usage, make sure you're aware of the ways they may circumvent parental restrictions.

By utilizing our technologies properly and being aware of the influence they have on us, we can maximize the way they operate for us instead of becoming slaves to them. We can increase our performance and take advantage of new chances. Slowly but slowly, our world will evolve into one that lives offline as well as online, blurring the borders of what's essential in life without being conscious of how we modify our priorities. I feel that re-evaluating how we utilize technology is vital to our well-being and our overall success as people and future leaders.

So far, we've discussed a lot about the bad aspects of technology and social media. But we don't only want to avoid the unpleasant. There's a largely positive aspect to it and you want to take advantage of it as well. (After all, a positive mindset makes you a better leader.)

Remember that just because everyone else is doing it does not imply that it is healthy! You can take advantage of technologies that promote your well-being, and you may restrict technologies that do not. If you feel that technology usage is badly impacting your life, or if other significant people in your life bring up concerns, it's appropriate to stand back and reevaluate your relationship with technology. What would you gain or lose by altering the way you utilize technology?

Chapter 4: You're more courageous than you know

You have more bravery than you realize. You will never know how courageous you are until you take that first step into your fear. The worst lie you will tell yourself is that you "can't." The first step is often the toughest. The ones that follow frequently lead to satisfaction and empowerment no matter what occurs. Just doing that hard thing can empower you and make you discover you have more guts than you know. Be bold and dare to be different.

Find role models of quietly brave individuals. I'm a strong believer in the value of role models for just about everything you aim to achieve or become. When you're attempting to expand yourself beyond your apparent boundaries, there's a part of you that questions if it can truly be done. A role model is a daily reminder that the answer is yes. Channel that person until it seems normal to channel your very own self. And if you don't have a role model nearby, consider Miep Gies, the modest and ordinary lady who housed Anne Frank in her attic for two years. "I don't want to be called a hero," stated Gies. "Imagine [if] young people would grow up with the sense that you had to be a hero to accomplish your human obligation. I am scared nobody will ever assist other people, since who is a hero? I was not. I was simply a regular housewife and secretary." In other words, practice being brave by conquering tiny worries like meeting new people or dining alone in a restaurant before you tackle anything like taking the lead on a school project or heading up your community's toy drive. By beginning small, you may grow acclimated to being bold without a lot of risks at first. Eventually, you will reach the point where you can take larger chances.

You question the current quo. Although you want to make sure you're not regarded as constantly being negative, you do want to question the status quo when appropriate. It's bold to provide alternative views to inspire new thinking among your friends and family. Positively present your opinions to avoid being considered a naysayer.

If you feel this situation sounds an awful lot like your life, you may want to go a bit further and decide the areas in your life where you may be bolder. For instance, it might be stressful to attempt to answer a question only to end up being incorrect. This may embarrass a lot of kids, but it shouldn't! If you are still studying the content, you shouldn't have all the answers, and giving it a chance is gutsy and important to learn. Here are some ideas to help you embrace bravery and incorporate it into your life.

Be yourself and be pleased with who you are. Dare to be the true you. Let them see you for who you are – errors, anxieties, and all. Insecurities are simpler to get through when we don't feel like we have to conceal them. Embrace your peculiarities instead of striving to be like someone else or behave in a manner that's not authentic to you. The idea is to concentrate on what you're enthusiastic about. If you're still attempting to find out what your burning wants are, consider asking your friends or family for their perspectives. When people think of you, what is it that they believe you're exceptional at? Discovering your abilities in connection to your passion is extremely significant since it indicates the direction you should pursue in life. Challenge yourself to try something that's slightly outside your regular comfort zone. Pick something you'd want to accomplish if only you had more confidence. Give yourself a little push and do it. Now that you've done that, select something new to try — and keep repeating this identical approach. Confidence builds with every stride forward.

Don’t ask yourself what you want out of life. It’s simple to desire prosperity and fame and happiness and fantastic sex. Everybody desires those goods. A far more intriguing question to ask oneself is, “What type of suffering do I want?” What you are willing to strive for is a stronger factor in how your lives turn out. Stay optimistic and have hope for the future. Stay on track even after encountering hurdles and anxieties. Instead of hiding, confront what is ahead. In many circumstances, fear is only in your brain. Most of what you dread will never come to pass. Don't spend time fretting when you can get ahead by living. The trick is to maintain your feet in the current moment. Whatever transpired is a matter of the past, something that cannot be altered. However, what you can alter is the way you respond to it now. Therefore, let go of your old moorings and open your mind to a more inquisitive, joyous attitude to life.

Continue to develop by continually attempting to learn and enhance your talents. Take every opportunity to master a new skill. Read the books of major thought leaders and learn all you can about being courageous. The more you know the less risk you have to undertake to be successful.

We gain character via those terrible moments. The adage, “what doesn’t kill me makes me stronger” is accurate. When you go through anything tough, you learn from it, regardless of the result. Recognize the potential for learning and personal growth

Chapter 5: It's okay to make mistakes

You will make mistakes, disappoint others, and fail terribly.

You should anticipate your life to experience some significant lows, big disappointments, and humiliating embarrassment. You are not immune to making errors. You will never be flawless, so prepare yourself for these falls and recognize that it's what you do with these low periods that counts. Give yourself an excess of grace when you goof up because while guilt and shame may be a good moral barometer, they can also damage your tranquility. Take responsibility for your acts and do all you can to rectify and redeem the situation. Remember that some of the best life lessons come from the toughest crashes. Sometimes growing hurts.

Identify your faults and learn from them. If you want to progress, instead of striving to make no errors at all, you should aim to make a new one each time. This implies that after you've made a mistake, you need to explore how to prevent it in the future. Take into consideration all that you have learned, and don't repeat what went wrong. When we don't learn from our errors, we impose extra stress on ourselves and others, and we risk losing people's faith and trust in us. In this post, we look at ways to guarantee that we take those lessons on board and then utilize what we learn.

Chances are, acting on what you've learned will take the discipline and determination to modify your behaviors, or to change the way that your team operates. Doing so will assist you to prevent self-sabotage in the future, and will allow you to realize the advantages and benefits of applying improved work habits. Use forgiveness as a technique to enhance your emotional well-being.

The most essential thing to remember is that you are so much more than your errors. Self-forgiveness is one of the most essential things you can do for yourself. Allow yourself to move on from the circumstances you wish you had handled differently and genuinely forgive yourself. These principles are challenging to adopt, but so is developing real self-forgiveness. It will most likely be a lengthy trip that will feature troughs and peaks. You may never totally release the unpleasant sentiments you have.

Self-forgiveness does not have to be self-indulgent, but rather a clear assessment of your ability for doing both good and wrong.

Have empathy for more than yourself. It has been shown that individuals have problems with self-forgiveness when they also feel empathy with the other person involved. It's typical for individuals to struggle with this tension. However, without feeling empathy towards both yourself and the other person, this self-forgiveness might be hollow and not signify anything. One of the silver linings of making a mistake, no matter how huge, is that you learn something from it. Try to acknowledge your blunders for helping taught you anything. You are the person you are today because of whatever mistake you made, and maybe it will help you become the person you want to be.

Be comfortable confessing you disappointed yourself, but find courage in knowing this one blunder doesn’t define you. Most essential, remember to be nice. Rather than obsessing or whipping yourself with guilt, practice self-compassion, which entails calming and guiding oneself like you would with a good friend. And besides, you can't recover in a punishing environment.”

Make modifications in your conduct to prevent similar incorrect circumstances and actions that caused you guilt in the past. Do not forget the lesson from the purported defeat. Consider what you might do differently today and start going in that direction. How can you be a better kid, a better friend, or a better person?

Chapter 6: Be cautious about how you judge success.

We live in a culture of mainstream media that typically defines success as beauty, fortune, and renown. Please don't trust these stats. Your success is dependent on your pleasure, contentment, and tranquility. Don't accept any other definition this world presents because it will just lead you down empty paths with a hungry heart.
What provides you profound joy?
What feeds your passion and fulfills your purpose?
What adds purpose to your life and pushes you to grow?
You will achieve genuine success if you pursue a life that addresses those questions. It is crucial to be cautious when judging success as a teenager.
We must deliberately analyze what is meant by "success", otherwise, we may drive

ourselves to match a restricted definition that may come in the way of flourishing in the long run. One must be aware to not incorrectly concentrate on two typical metrics of success - the grin on their faces and the grades they obtain in school.
What's wrong with gauging success by grades? They measure just one facet of a person's efforts. Grades could make young people feel inept rather than enable them to recognize abilities they possess in areas ungraded. When we assess achievement by academics, kids may estimate their value by what they have accomplished by age 18. This diminishes the capacity to realize that life provides ongoing possibilities for development and self-improvement. They could feel as if they have "failed" solely because they have not secured placement in the college or training program of choice. When youth internalize pressure to get grades, it may impede the development of

some of the key character characteristics that predict long-term success.

While happiness is the greatest measure of success for many youths, 1 in 10 respondents (10 percent) say that accomplishing one's objectives is one method to attain success. One 13-year-old child argues that a successful person achieves "everything they set out [to] does in life. People's aims are varied, but as long as they attain that goal I believe they are successful."

Counting your blessings might be a better approach to assessing your progress. The reason establishing how you spend your time each day is a true measure of success is that this informs you whether you have been able to delegate and develop an efficient organization, and it establishes what your major priorities ought to be as the head of a firm. I tend to work all the time, but what I found is that I might be more effective by prioritizing duties and letting go of some of the less critical chores. I could let others take the lead, which turns them into a terrific, trusted team.

Count your blessings. When you recognize how precious you really are and how much you have to go for you, the smiles will reappear, the sun will shine, the music will play, and you will finally be able to move ahead toward the life that God planned for you... with elegance, power, boldness, and confidence.

Spreading love and showing grace to others may also be a measure of success. When you understand how unjust the world is, you realize how much you need to serve people regardless of their background. Rather than adopting a selfish posture, you regard spreading charity and mercy to others as an opportunity.

There are many different sorts of success and it is crucial to pick the proper metric for you.

There is no one measure of success and definitely no single solution for how to be successful in life. Yet by studying some of the behaviors of successful individuals, you might discover new methods and ideas to adopt in your own everyday life. Cultivate and cultivate these qualities, and over time you may discover that you are better able to attain your objectives and achieve the success you seek in life.

For many individuals, metrics of success are a highly relative subject. If you're wondering if you're succeeding, you may try glancing around at others who have a similar background to yourself. This might imply folks with comparable credentials, those of a similar age, or just your buddies. If you see that most of your similar peers are achieving more than you, this might drive you to strive more. If they're your buddies, ask them what they do and for more comments. If you discover that you're performing better than others, you know that you're doing the proper thing.

We live in a culture of mainstream media that typically defines success as beauty, fortune, and renown. Please don’t trust these stats. Your success is dependent on your pleasure, contentment, and tranquility. Don’t accept any other definition this world presents because it will just lead you down empty paths with a hungry heart. What provides you profound joy? What feeds your passion and fulfills your purpose? What adds purpose to your life and pushes you to grow? If you live a life that answers those questions, you will achieve genuine success.

Chapter 7: Avoid Violence

Schools play a vital part in the creation of the young person's foundation for constructing a life and it is acceptable to anticipate that the spaces for learning should be safe.
Unfortunately, this is not always the case, since, in many situations, classrooms may become "war zones". In the recent decade, 284 youngsters were slain due to school violence — these included shootings, stabbings, fights, and suicides.
Create healthy and pleasant connections with others.
Prioritize the friendship above winning.
Many individuals approach a fight with the purpose of "winning." Unfortunately, this merely produces more friction and may damage your relationship. The first step to healthily resolving conflict is to attempt to understand the other person's point of view so that you can work together to establish a mutually acceptable solution. Everyone

participating should be able to express their point of view and explain their demands, produce a list of viable solutions, and pick an option that fulfills as many needs as feasible and is acceptable to everyone. It's actually about adjusting our perspective from characterizing the fight as "me versus you" to "you and I against the problem."

Pick your fights. Conflicts may be taxing, so it's crucial to examine if the problem is worth your time and energy. If you can let the tiny things slip, you will have more harmonious relationships with others and the people in your life will pay more attention when you are unhappy about the larger things.

Be mindful of your responses and reactions to conflict - You can inflame the situation without trying to, for example, by yelling or reacting back with hostility. Keep yourself cool. Leave the room for a time if you need to. Respond rather than react.

Teenagers must learn about healthy conflict resolution and conflict resolution skills. Conflicts are a part of life, and so, conflict resolution skills for teens are crucial to help them cope with things more effectively. Teens are an age during which there are a lot of hormonal and emotional changes occurring in the body. These changes make temper outbursts, confrontation, and lashing out other frequent adolescent behavior qualities. Good conflict resolution skills are some of the most helpful talents you can master as a teenager. These abilities may help you develop healthy relationships, reduce violence, set you up for excellent work, and overall be more successful in life.

Chapter 8: Learn to manage stress and time

Stress & Time Management

Managing the pressure to excel in every aspect of life and finding time to accomplish it all appears to be one of the main issues confronting the young today. Young people are expected to be successful, however, few of them are aware of excellent time management.

Stress and time management tips for adolescents:

Learn to control stress.

Think about what you have to complete soon, and come up with an action plan to lead you through the burden with little stress. Don't let vital duties pile up since they'll be more unpleasant to address in a time-crunched circumstance.

Reach out. Build a network of pals that help you cope in a good manner. Talk to trustworthy adults or friends that will listen to you and not criticize you or overreact. Talking about stress may help you voice emotions, feel validated, and may help you get started tackling your situation.

Let go of perfection. Try to appreciate things as they are, not as you believe they should be. Learn to feel good about accomplishing a competent or "good enough" job rather than seeking perfection from yourself and others. It's necessary to push yourself to accomplish your best, but perfection is typically not feasible. Accept family and friends for who they are, even if they may not meet all of your expectations.

Manage time more efficiently.

The trick? Find a decent time management system and work it. There are numerous. It's totally up to you which one you chose. But if you don't want to become part of the 92 percent figure of individuals who fail to reach their long-term objectives, then you need to pay attention to how you utilize the relatively little time you do have in this world.

You may not believe that this would assist you in better managing your time, but meditating and exercising every single morning provides you with balance. Cut the pollutants out of your life and become serious by doing this and watch as your energy, stamina and mental concentration take a radical leap.

Combine chores and errands for time efficiency. For example, while creating a meal for yourself, create more than one dish; eat one serving now and preserve the remainder for later. Also, while organizing your day or even your week, establish what errands you have to do and work out which ones you can consolidate into one trip. Set small objectives to accomplish everyday productivity.

Every evening before bed, prepare a list for the following day. Look at your objectives and see what you can do to assist and take you closer. This doesn't happen overnight. It takes time. But by generating to-do lists, you're setting objectives for the day. Daily objectives are easy to attain while helping to propel us towards longer and greater goals. But that occurs via generating to-do lists. So if you're serious about accomplishing your objectives, not only do you need to establish those goals properly, but you also have to become serious about avoiding distractions and being too entrenched in the bad habits that you know you need to abandon. Time-wasters need to go by the wayside, and true grit-and-bear-it hard labor has to take its place.

There's a proper and incorrect method to establish objectives. If you don't properly establish your objectives, then you'll lack the necessary targets, which will push you to slip off course. But when you position them the proper way, the sky's the limit. Use the SMART goal-setting approach to help you see things through. And when you do create those objectives, make sure you have tremendous deep down reasons for wanting to reach them.

Chapter 9: Not all that glitters is gold

Materialism

We live in a world that fosters materialism and young people are taught to assess success and pleasure in life primarily on how much good they have. A materialistic attitude toward life may result in discontent when one doesn't have enough and can severely affect a person's life.

Advice on materialism for adolescents:

Teens nowadays are presented with a whole new level of consumerism.

Today's teens have been labeled as the most materialistic generation in history. Many kids are highly status-conscious, and to increase their position among their classmates, they feel driven to purchase the newest technology or the "cool" brand names. Their self-worth is motivated by their things. Ultimately, this sort of attitude may lead to bad financial choices and debt and an underlying discontent with their lives.

"Particularly relevant," added John, "is the fact that by just improving self-esteem in teenagers, we notice a reduced reliance on material objects that mimics that of young children. While friends and marketing may surely impact youth, consumerism is strongly tied to self-esteem."

A poll was performed some years ago of youngsters from seventy cities in more than fifteen nations. The findings from our nation indicated that 75 percent of U.S. tweens (children ages 8-12) want to be affluent; 61 percent want to be famous, and the majority of youngsters in the U.S. feel the brand of their clothing defines who they are. If these results can be applied to other young people in our nation, it would suggest many are already entrenched in materialistic attitudes.

As an emerging value, materialism helps explain the buying behavior of youth. Using a nationwide sample of 9- to 14-year-olds, in this research we established a Youth Materialism Scale. The data show that more materialistic youngsters are likely to buy more and save less. They are most interested in new items and most attentive to advertising and promotional activities. Their parents consider them more knowledgeable about items, and they have more purchasing power over their parents. More materialistic parents are likely to spawn more materialistic children. This research also demonstrates a small negative link between materialism and love for the school and school achievement.
Ways to cope with consumerism in teens.
Be supportive. Recent research indicated that teens with supportive parents and friends had stronger self-esteem, which makes them less materialistic. Youngsters with lower self-esteem valued goods substantially more

than children with stronger self-esteem. So, parents, be supportive of your children. Your first step towards that might be reading our prior blog, Building Confidence in Teens. Establish objectives and challenges. Many individuals may attempt to use items to fill a gap inside themselves. The difficulty is that "stuff" can't accomplish that. Teach your adolescent to set their objectives and challenges so that they may base their self-worth on their activities rather than their belongings or the adoration of their peers. Inspiring youth to seek lives of higher significance – a life not defined by their belongings but by their deeds and goals – may very well save them financial strain and false promises of bliss. It is difficult to keep kids out of the materialistic trap because of our society's expanding culture of "buying more", the targeted advertising to teens and young adults, and teens need to fit in with their classmates. However, their spending habits are not entirely set — parents and other adults have the power to mold their thinking and choices on materialism before they get themselves into debt or in other difficulties.

Chapter 10: You're enough the way you are.

How to overcome a bad image as teenagers:

Identify your image and how to enhance it. Take attention to all of the things your body can perform. You may be able to enhance your body image by concentrating more on what it can accomplish instead of what it looks like. Even if you are not sporty, think about how you utilize your body every day. One of the finest recommendations for how to enhance body image is to start viewing your body from a positive perspective, instead of a negative or neutral one. Every person's body has great possibilities, even if you feel constrained by it at times. It's crucial to concentrate on what your body can accomplish. Cultivate thankfulness for your body's talents.

Focus on what you enjoy about your physique. Identifying your preferred traits may enable you to establish a more positive body image. Take a few seconds each day to look at yourself in the mirror and pick your favorite characteristics of your physique. Be mindful of the media's influence in altering your body image. We are continually assaulted with pictures of "ideal" beauty and taught that we are defective. Recognize that these messages are being utilized to sell you a product and that they have no foundation in reality. The photographs of models and performers that you see in publications are routinely edited to make them seem immaculate. Know that this unachievable ideal of beauty may be hurting your body image. Identify reasons you wish to enhance your body image. To improve the way that you think about your body, consider some of the advantages that you intend to receive as a consequence of a more positive body image. Write these positives down so that you remember them.

Self-image is not fixed. Part of our self-image is dynamic and evolving. We may learn to establish a healthier and more true perspective of ourselves, therefore addressing the distortions in the mirror. Self-image transformation happens during a lifetime. A good self-image begins with learning to accept and appreciate oneself. It also implies being welcomed and liked by others. Use your mirror to boost your body image. While your mirror may also be a tool for you to critique your body, you may learn to utilize your mirror to enhance your body image. Every time you look at yourself in the mirror, find something that you enjoy about your appearance and express it out loud.

Consider problems that have contributed to your body image. Understanding the problems that you have endured that may have led to your poor body image may assist you. Try to recall any specific problems that may have led to the development of any of the thoughts and attitudes you have about your body. Refocusing your self-talk is a wonderful place to start. Rather than obsessing about your body's looks, consider noticing and appreciating the fantastic things it accomplishes for you every day. For instance, appreciate that your strong and big hands allow you to handle the basketball conveniently. Or that your expert hands created an excellent feast. Familiarise yourself with social media networks. You may already have a Facebook or Instagram account, but do you understand how people communicate on Snapchat or TikTok? The more you grasp these platforms, the simpler it will be to recognize anything that’s not right.

How to cope with peer pressure and unfavorable image.

Chapter 11: Overcoming Peer Pressure

Get guidance from an adult. If you confront peer pressure that's hard to manage, obtain guidance from an adult you trust. Talk to a parent, teacher, or school counselor. It may make you feel considerably better. Plus, they may help you prepare for the next time you experience peer pressure.

Walk away. If you're confronted with peer pressure when you're alone, there are still things you can do. You can keep away from peers who urge you to do what you know is improper. You may tell them, "Nah" and walk away. Better still, locate other friends and classmates to hang out with.

Teach extra resistance tactics. When confronting negative peer pressure, asking leading questions or making targeted remarks may occasionally change the emphasis or force a reassessment. Other times, establishing a scapegoat may be useful, so give yourself up as their reason for not following ahead with the plan or yielding to pressure.

Have a buddy who will stand with you. It may assist to have at least one other peer who is willing to say "No," too. This takes a lot of strength out of peer pressure. It's important to have people that will back you up when you don't want to do anything. Teens who mistrust their talents, judgment, or self-worth are more inclined to submit to negative peer pressure. Continue to assist yourself develop your capacity to identify good from wrong, and gain confidence to trust in this skill.

Peer pressure is a huge concern for teenagers and young adults. Even if you strive hard to combat it, you may find yourself falling under pressure from friends or classmates. You could go along with just about anything to avoid being dubbed a “loser” or “scared-y cat.” Those labels may be no fun, but giving in to social pressure means moving away

from your own identity in favor of someone else's. Learn how to avoid peer pressure and live according to your ideals.
Start the dialogue early with any trustworthy adult. People of all ages encounter bouts of peer pressure, but the adolescent years appear to be especially fertile for it. The urge to "fit in" or impress others is at a high peak, which may lead to both good and bad actions. It is safer to presume that every youngster will suffer negative peer pressure and to speak about it well in advance. Dealing with (and handing out) peer pressure is a rite of passage for teens. Positive types of social pressure may stimulate positive outcomes (like excellent grades) or positive activities (like volunteering), while bad peer pressure can lead to dangerous behaviors, poor performance, and lower self-esteem. Helping teens overcome negative peer pressure might begin before they are even teenagers, but it's never too late to start the process. When you

do pursue it, employ active communication, demonstration of appropriate avoidance and coping skills, and support of self-worth.
Take notice of the fact that the biggest peer pressure is likely to come from friends – true friends, deceptive friends, and new friends.
Be encouraged to pick carefully and constantly review the total worth of each connection.
Peer pressure may be beneficial or detrimental. When peer pressure is good, it motivates you to be your best. Negative peer pressure occurs when a friend or member of a group you belong to makes you feel as if you must do something to be accepted. It's the negative peer pressure that we normally think of when the word peer pressure is used.
When you give in to negative peer pressure, you typically feel guilty or unhappy with yourself for behaving in a manner that goes against your ideas or ideals.

Chapter 12: Think it through before saying or doing anything

Do your research before responding to conflicts. This is the ultimate goal—to agree on an alternative that helps both parties to some degree. When one side wins via violent conduct or one party just gives up, someone is losing. And it means you obtain results that do not fix the core reasons for the dispute.

It's worth selecting your fights. If you can be flexible about tiny matters, you may be able to avoid some confrontation. So even if you despise your friend's joke, think about whether it's worth fighting over. This can suggest your buddy is more open to listening and addressing major topics like safety.

Here's an approach that works:

Step 1. Think about a disagreement you're experiencing. What is it about? Who is it with? How do you feel about it? What steps do you wish to take? Take a few minutes to jot down your responses to the preceding questions. This may help you process your ideas and emotions better. Before going on to the next phase, genuinely attempt to grasp what's underneath the struggle you're feeling.

Be mindful that dispute resolution is not a one-size-fits-all. Depending on the person(s) involved and the circumstances related to the dispute, each conflict will need to be addressed differently. It should also be stated that disagreements are not usually settled at the drop of a hat—it is a process, one that needs time and patience on behalf of both sides. Be mindful that, just like any key skill, resolving a disagreement is tough, and it's good to fumble along the way.

From the school yard to the house, we confront conflict at every stage of our lives. The capacity to overcome problems with one another is an essential life skill, particularly in today's polarized environment. Instead of waiting for someone to tell you to "calm down," display the right conduct. Try to see the numerous approaches for relaxing. It might be as easy as taking a brief "cool down" minute to assess your feelings before responding. Some find jogging, reading, or sketching to be beneficial strategies for diverting negative energy. Whatever the situation may be, the takeaway here is that nothing beneficial can come from hasty, emotional responses during a fight. Know that a sensible dialogue is always more useful than a heated fight.

Consider the other person's viewpoint before responding: Listen to the opposing point of view. Being a good listener is a means of expressing that you appreciate and understand the other person's viewpoint. That makes it much more likely he or she will do the same for you. Try not to worry about why you disagree or what you'll say next while the other person is speaking. Instead, concentrate on what's being said. When it's your moment to speak, repeat any major points the other person made to demonstrate you listened and heard what was stated. Then calmly give your position and why you disagree. Avoid bringing down the other person's thoughts and opinions. If you've ever been on the receiving end of someone's diatribe or put-downs, you know how useful utilizing courteous language and conduct can be. So instead of stating what you may be thinking ("That's a bad idea!"), try: "I don't agree, and here's why." Resist the impulse to shout, use sarcasm, or make nasty remarks and you'll have a lot higher chance of getting your message through.

Perspective taking depends not only upon our ability to communicate feelings with others but also upon our skill to manage our own emotions. To be productive with others we must be mindful of what can trigger us so we can swiftly refocus ourselves on what is occurring with the other. When it comes to empathy, the objective is not to ask ourselves what we would do in any particular scenario; it's to try to comprehend what another would do.

Chapter 13: Accessing accurate information about others:

Often, to effectively assess another person's point of view, we will want extra knowledge about the individual, some of which we may deduce from our contacts with the person. But be cautious, we frequently acquire a lot of incorrect impressions about people, so it’s necessary to carefully analyze the information you’re using to judge the other person’s point of view.

Step 2: Think about what’s troubling you from the viewpoint of the person(s) you’re disagreeing with. How do you believe they perceive the conflict? How do you suppose they feel about it? What were their intentions? Take a few minutes to write about the disagreement from the other person(s) viewpoint.

Now look at the photo again and assume that you are the guy holding the pistol. Imagine that you’re in the circumstances you stated.

Take a fresh piece of paper and retell the scenario from the viewpoint of the guy with the gun. What is he thinking or feeling? Spend around three minutes doing this. Perspective taking takes the maturity to gather information and be tolerant of another person's particular ideas. Disrespect for another person and their belief system is the easiest way to create alienation and division amongst individuals. It is the surest method to anger a friend, classmate, or even family. Social judgment complicates the social environment and it's something we ALL do. We can't help but make estimates and develop social judgments about others' motives and people doing the same to us. Those who adjust what they do and say as a method to maintain others have "acceptable" or "neutral" ideas are significantly more likely to be deemed friendly than when someone acts or says anything that causes "mixed" social memory. In teaching social

perspective taking, we assist social learners first to understand they have their social judgments and recollections about how what other people said or did make them feel (good and negative) (positive and negative). We learn that we all modify what we do and say not only for what's occurring in the present but also depending on how we hope others will remember our actions and emotions in the future. We often question conference participants why, while feeling irritated in meetings or classes, they don't immediately shout at others. The reaction is the same again and time, regardless of color, gender, age, or culture. Most of us don't do or say everything we feel at the time because we know that others will have confusing, or bad social memories of the incident, which will likely result in future encounters.
Adjusting from an egocentric default: The most fundamental component of viewing things from someone else's point of view is

being able to see beyond your viewpoint. This may be quite tough since your perspective is instantaneous, natural, and effortless. In contrast, reasoning about another person's mental state is slow, methodical, and challenging. It is crucial to be extremely attentive to the reality that not all individuals share our particular perspectives and opinions about the world. We must be open-minded and sensitive to what others think while interacting with them. This involves knowing what not to say as much as knowing what to say. This makes communication challenging, but it keeps you open and learning in the process of being able to set yourself aside and be respectful of others.

Conclusion

When you turn on others to determine your worth, you are dismissing your talents, physical qualities, and voice. Honor who you were designed to be, and spend your life embracing your distinctive traits and unique sense of purpose. Think about what you can do for other people and what sort of person you want to be. Focus on it instead of what everyone else is doing. Choose friends who are trustworthy, helpful, and compassionate. Find folks that share a lot of your hobbies - you should have some comparable interests. Be honest with yourself about how comfortable you feel among your buddies. Join a club, take a class or join an organization that focuses on something you are passionate about. Be yourself and be a nice friend to someone you have a lot in common with. Look for groups that cluster around an interest or hobby you share.

Connect with others who have similar interests and develop meaningful relationships with them. Spend time with your mates. Create a healthy relationship with technology by knowing how you use it. Use a calendar or planning tool to keep track of chores and obligations. Engage in physical activity several times a week to help release excessive stress. If you're monitoring your children's internet activity, make sure you're aware of the methods they may use to avoid parental limits. I believe that re-evaluating how we employ technology is crucial to our well-being and our overall success as individuals and future leaders. Gauge how much time you're spending on each application and change your strategy properly.

If you want to develop, instead of attempting to make no mistakes at all, you should seek to create a new one each time. Take responsibility for your deeds and do everything you can to fix and redeem the situation. Self-forgiveness is one of the most fundamental things you can do for yourself. Remember that some of the finest life lessons come from the worst wrecks. Be comfortable saying you disappointed yourself, but find bravery in knowing this one misstep doesn't define you.

Instead of fretting or lashing yourself with guilt, practice self-compassion, which means soothing and guiding oneself like a good friend. Consider what you may do differently today and start heading in that direction. It is vital to be careful when measuring success as a teenager and understand what it means to be a success. Your success depends on your joy, satisfaction, and tranquility. How you use your time each day is a genuine indicator of your success. You will attain true success if you follow a life that answers those issues.

To scale through the challenges and difficulties of a teenage hood, one needs to face the challenges as his or herself and above all look up to people that are experienced for guidance. There is no better way to do this than seeking guardians from elderly ones, especially our parents. In that way, mistakes will be reduced, and even when they are made you can easily learn from them. You say life is not always rosy. Some things happen for us to learn from them. They go a long way to ensure that we avoid all the ugly situations that can result in the future. Teenagers, therefore, need to be purposeful in their dealings with other peers in their daily lives. Bear at the back of your mind that life is just one and you can live to your fullest potential if you do it your way and not by imitating others and also bicycle guardians from those that I've been in your shoes. Is looking up to the elderly ones for advice and guardians. Finally do not forget that you are who you are and not who people see you be and you are enough the way you are.

www.ingramcontent.com/pod-product-compliance
Lightning Source LLC
LaVergne TN
LVHW052056160826
845678LV00015B/3254
9798847523233